What if we do NTHING?

# OBESITY

## Michaela Miller

FRANKLIN WATTS
LONDON•SYDNEY

First published in 2006 by
Franklin Watts
338 Euston Road
London NW1 3BH

Franklin Watts Australia
Hachette Children's Books
Level 17/207 Kent St, Sydney, NSW 2000

Produced by Arcturus Publishing Limited,
26/27 Bickels Yard, 151-153 Bermondsey Street, London SE1 3HA

Series concept: Alex Woolf
Editor: Alex Woolf
Designer: Peta Morey
Picture researcher: Glass Onion Pictures
Consultant: Kathleen L. Keller, PhD, New York Obesity Research Center

Picture Credits
Corbis: 10 (Karen Kasmauski), 17 (Pat Doyle), 19 (Mark Peterson), 33 (Peter Turnley),
34 (Anders Ryman), 42 (Don Mason), 45 (Mark Ralston/Reuters).
Rex: 7 (David Lissy), 22 (John Powell), 39 (Sipa Press).
Science Photo Library: 4 (Simon Fraser), 8 (Steve Gschmeissner), 12 (Marcelo
Brodsky), 14 (Mark Clarke), 21 (BSIP VEM), 26 (David Munns), 29 (National Cancer
Institute), 36 (Peter Menzel).
TopFoto: 25 (Bob Daemmrich/The Image Works), 31 (Ellen B. Senisi/The Image Works),
40 (Michael J. Doolittle/The Image Works).

A CIP catalogue record for this book is available from the British Library

Dewey Decimal Classification Number: 616.3'98

ISBN 07496 6615 3

Printed in China

# Contents

CHAPTER 1
**What is Obesity?** 4

CHAPTER 2
**What Causes Obesity?** 11

CHAPTER 3
**Obesity and Health** 18

CHAPTER 4
**Obesity in Children and Young People** 24

CHAPTER 5
**Obesity in the Developing World** 32

CHAPTER 6
**Creating a Healthy Future** 38

**Glossary and Further Information** 46

**Debate Panel answers** 47

**Index** 48

# What is Obesity?

**The year is 2020.** Sophie has little energy. She is constantly thirsty and tired all the time. Walking up the stairs in her house is such an effort these days. Sophie is just 14 years old and lives in England. She has diabetes, which started because she was so overweight. Her doctor has told her she must take her insulin, change her diet and exercise more, but Sophie watches about eight hours of television a day, hates exercise and can't stop eating chocolate and crisps.

Her mother is desperate. She knows Sophie could die because of the health problems caused by obesity. The family has little money and they don't know how much longer they will be able to pay for insulin. There are now so many obese diabetics that the health service is running out of money and will not pay for Sophie's treatment.

In 2020 one third of adults in the UK are obese. The health problems associated with diabetes – kidney failure, blindness and loss of limbs caused by circulation problems are on the rise. Children now have a lower life expectancy than their parents...

### Obesity – the facts

Obesity is a medical disorder in which someone has so much extra body fat that it affects their health and ability to live normally. It causes many health problems including heart disease, diabetes and certain cancers.

To find out if an adult is obese, doctors and scientists use the body mass index (BMI). The BMI is a calculation that shows if someone is underweight, the normal weight, or overweight or obese. The BMIs for overweight and obesity are defined by the World Health Organization and are calculated by dividing a person's weight in kilograms by their height in metres squared.

A doctor discusses the need to lose weight with an obese patient. The patient may suffer from a range of health problems if he does not reach his target weight.

For example, a person who is 1.65 metres tall and weighs 64 kilograms has a BMI of 24.

People with a BMI of between 25 and 30 are said to be overweight, while those with a BMI of 30 or more are classified as obese. Someone within the normal weight range should have a BMI of between 18.5 and 24.9 while anyone with a BMI of less than 18.5 is underweight. Generally, a man who is 16 to 18 kilograms overweight for his height, and a woman who is 13.5 kilograms overweight for her height, would be described as obese.

$$\frac{64\text{kg}}{1.65\text{m}^2} = 24$$

**To calculate a person's body mass index, take the weight in kilograms and divide it by the height in metres squared.**

**This chart can be used to work out an adult's body mass index. Find the intersection of weight and height. This gives the BMI.**

Height (centimetres)

| Weight (kilograms) | 150 | 152.5 | 155 | 157.5 | 160 | 162.5 | 165 | 167.5 | 170 | 172.5 | 175 | 177.5 | 180 | 182.5 | 185 | 187.5 | 190 | Weight (pounds) |
|---|---|---|---|---|---|---|---|---|---|---|---|---|---|---|---|---|---|---|
| 45 | 20 | 19 | 18 | 18 | 17 | 17 | 16 | 16 | 15 | 15 | 14 | 14 | 14 | 13 | 13 | 12 | 12 | 100 |
| 47 | 21 | 20 | 19 | 19 | 18 | 17 | 17 | 16 | 16 | 16 | 15 | 15 | 14 | 14 | 13 | 13 | 13 | 105 |
| 50 | 22 | 21 | 20 | 19 | 19 | 18 | 18 | 17 | 17 | 16 | 16 | 15 | 15 | 15 | 14 | 14 | 13 | 110 |
| 52 | 23 | 22 | 21 | 20 | 20 | 19 | 19 | 18 | 17 | 17 | 17 | 16 | 16 | 15 | 15 | 14 | 14 | 115 |
| 54 | 23 | 23 | 22 | 21 | 21 | 20 | 19 | 19 | 18 | 18 | 17 | 17 | 16 | 16 | 15 | 15 | 15 | 120 |
| 57 | 24 | 24 | 23 | 22 | 21 | 21 | 20 | 20 | 19 | 18 | 18 | 17 | 17 | 16 | 16 | 16 | 15 | 125 |
| 59 | 25 | 25 | 24 | 23 | 22 | 22 | 21 | 20 | 20 | 19 | 19 | 18 | 18 | 17 | 17 | 16 | 16 | 130 |
| 61 | 26 | 26 | 25 | 24 | 23 | 22 | 22 | 21 | 21 | 20 | 19 | 19 | 18 | 18 | 17 | 17 | 16 | 135 |
| 63 | 27 | 26 | 26 | 25 | 24 | 23 | 23 | 22 | 21 | 21 | 20 | 20 | 19 | 18 | 18 | 17 | 17 | 140 |
| 66 | 28 | 27 | 27 | 26 | 25 | 24 | 23 | 23 | 22 | 21 | 21 | 20 | 20 | 19 | 19 | 18 | 18 | 145 |
| 68 | 29 | 28 | 27 | 27 | 26 | 25 | 24 | 23 | 23 | 22 | 22 | 21 | 20 | 20 | 19 | 19 | 18 | 150 |
| 70 | 30 | 29 | 28 | 27 | 27 | 26 | 25 | 24 | 24 | 23 | 22 | 22 | 21 | 20 | 20 | 19 | 19 | 155 |
| 72 | 31 | 30 | 29 | 28 | 27 | 27 | 26 | 25 | 24 | 24 | 23 | 22 | 22 | 21 | 21 | 20 | 19 | 160 |
| 75 | 32 | 31 | 30 | 29 | 28 | 27 | 27 | 26 | 25 | 24 | 24 | 23 | 22 | 22 | 21 | 21 | 20 | 165 |
| 77 | 33 | 32 | 31 | 30 | 29 | 28 | 27 | 27 | 26 | 25 | 24 | 24 | 23 | 22 | 22 | 21 | 21 | 170 |
| 79 | 34 | 33 | 32 | 31 | 30 | 29 | 28 | 27 | 27 | 26 | 25 | 24 | 24 | 23 | 22 | 22 | 21 | 175 |
| 82 | 35 | 34 | 33 | 32 | 31 | 30 | 29 | 28 | 27 | 27 | 26 | 25 | 24 | 24 | 23 | 22 | 22 | 180 |
| 84 | 36 | 35 | 34 | 33 | 32 | 31 | 30 | 29 | 28 | 27 | 27 | 26 | 25 | 24 | 24 | 23 | 23 | 185 |
| 86 | 37 | 36 | 35 | 34 | 33 | 32 | 31 | 30 | 29 | 28 | 27 | 26 | 26 | 25 | 24 | 24 | 23 | 190 |
| 88 | 38 | 37 | 36 | 35 | 33 | 32 | 31 | 31 | 30 | 29 | 28 | 27 | 26 | 26 | 25 | 24 | 24 | 195 |
| 91 | 39 | 38 | 37 | 35 | 34 | 33 | 32 | 31 | 30 | 30 | 29 | 28 | 27 | 26 | 26 | 25 | 24 | 200 |
| 93 | 40 | 39 | 37 | 36 | 35 | 34 | 33 | 32 | 31 | 30 | 29 | 29 | 28 | 27 | 26 | 26 | 25 | 205 |
| 95 | 41 | 40 | 38 | 37 | 36 | 35 | 34 | 33 | 32 | 31 | 30 | 29 | 28 | 28 | 27 | 26 | 26 | 210 |
| 98 | 42 | 41 | 39 | 38 | 37 | 36 | 35 | 34 | 33 | 32 | 31 | 30 | 29 | 28 | 28 | 27 | 26 | 215 |
| 100 | 43 | 42 | 40 | 39 | 38 | 37 | 36 | 34 | 33 | 32 | 32 | 31 | 30 | 29 | 28 | 27 | 27 | 220 |
| 102 | 44 | 43 | 41 | 40 | 39 | 37 | 36 | 35 | 34 | 33 | 32 | 31 | 31 | 30 | 29 | 28 | 27 | 225 |
| 104 | 45 | 43 | 42 | 41 | 39 | 38 | 37 | 36 | 35 | 34 | 33 | 32 | 31 | 30 | 30 | 29 | 28 | 230 |
| 107 | 46 | 44 | 43 | 42 | 40 | 39 | 38 | 37 | 36 | 35 | 34 | 33 | 32 | 31 | 30 | 29 | 29 | 235 |
| 109 | 47 | 45 | 44 | 43 | 41 | 40 | 39 | 38 | 36 | 35 | 34 | 33 | 33 | 32 | 31 | 30 | 29 | 240 |
| 111 | 48 | 46 | 45 | 43 | 42 | 41 | 40 | 38 | 37 | 36 | 35 | 34 | 33 | 32 | 31 | 31 | 30 | 245 |
| 114 | 49 | 47 | 46 | 44 | 43 | 42 | 40 | 39 | 38 | 37 | 36 | 35 | 34 | 33 | 32 | 31 | 30 | 250 |
| | 5'0" | 5'1" | 5'2" | 5'3" | 5'4" | 5'5" | 5'6" | 5'7" | 5'8" | 5'9" | 5'10" | 5'11" | 6'0" | 6'1" | 6'2" | 6'3" | 6'4" | |

Height (feet and inches)

Key — Underweight — Normal weight — Overweight — Obese

Source: Obesity: Third Report of Session 2003-04 by the House of Commons Health Committee, 2004, page 131

World Health Organization guidelines also use waist measurements to show if someone is obese. A man with a waist measurement of over 94 centimetres and a woman with a waist measurement of over 80 centimetres can be considered obese. This is called central obesity measurement.

Researchers have found that health problems caused by obesity can occur at different BMIs for people of different ethnic origin. For example, an overweight Asian man with a BMI of 27.5 or more is likely to suffer from the same incidences of health problems and increased risk of death as a Caucasian man with a BMI of 30.

## Energy in – energy out

How do we gain extra weight? One of the simplest explanations is to look at the energy we put into our bodies and the energy that we use up through different activities. The body needs energy to work effectively and it gets its energy from food. If a person is active they will use up more energy than someone who is inactive.

The energy within food and that we use up in our everyday lives is normally measured in kilojoules and kilocalories (calories for short). One kilojoule equals 1,000 joules of energy and one calorie equals 4.1868 joules. When referring to the energy values of food and the energy used up doing various activities, the calorie is the most commonly used unit of measurement.

## COUNTING CALORIES

Different types of food contain different amounts of calories. For example, an average-sized apple contains about 53 calories, a chocolate bar may contain around 290 calories, and 200 grams of grilled chicken breast without the skin contains around 232 calories. Oil, butter, sauces – anything we might put on our food or that it is cooked in – contain calories too. Chocolate bars, cakes and biscuits that contain a lot of fats and sugars contain more calories than foods like vegetables, fruit and grilled meat of equivalent weights.

To stay at the same weight, a normally active man of average height, weighing 74 kilograms, and aged between 19 and 50, needs to take in about 2,550 calories a day. A normally active woman of average height, weighing 64 kilograms, and aged between 19 and 50, needs 1,940 calories. If someone takes in more calories than they use up, the calories (the unused energy) are stored in their bodies as fat. Taller people usually need to take in more energy than smaller ones.

**Active people like this runner use up more calories than those people who are inactive. If someone takes in more calories than they actually use they will gain weight.**

### Burning energy

Different types of activities burn off different amounts of calories. To burn off the 294 calories contained in a chocolate bar, an average-sized man aged 25 would have to walk moderately quickly for 59 minutes.

7

To burn off the chocolate bar more quickly the man could play tennis, jog or dig for 47 minutes. The fastest way to burn off the calories in the chocolate bar would be to play football or swim front crawl for 39 minutes.

## A matter of fat

When calories are not burned off they are stored in the body as fat. It takes 3,500 unused calories to create one pound of body fat. This fat can be burned off if a person becomes more active and uses more energy, but if it is never burned off and more fat is stored, a person's BMI rises and they become overweight and eventually obese.

Fat is stored in cells which stop being created in the body at the end of puberty. Fat cells get bigger or smaller depending on the amount of fat stored within them. Because overweight and obese children may have up to three times more fat cells in their bodies than children of normal weight, it is harder for them to lose weight. Even when they are adults they will still have the same number of fat cells within their bodies. They will never be able to get rid of the actual cells, only the fat within them.

## Fat storage

Most fat is stored under the skin, but it is stored in different areas depending on whether you are male or female. Adult men tend to store fat around their chests, waists and buttocks, giving them an apple shape when they are overweight or obese. Adult females usually store fat around their breasts, waists, hips and chests, producing more of a pear shape. In both men and women, some fat is stored around the kidneys and inside the liver and muscles.

This image from a powerful microscope shows fat cells that are stored under the skin. Fat cells get bigger or smaller depending on the amount of fat within them.

Not all fat is bad – it is very important for humans to have some fat, otherwise our bodies will not work properly.

## A worldwide problem

Obesity is on the increase all around the globe. The World Health Organization estimated that in 1995 there were 200 million obese people in the world. By 2002 the number had risen to 300 million.

Obesity is traditionally associated with the richer countries in the developed world. In the USA approximately 130 million adults are overweight or obese, and in the UK one fifth of all adults are obese. In most European countries the incidence of obesity has increased by between 10 and 40 per cent over the past ten years.

**This chart shows obesity levels for men and women in 29 European countries.**

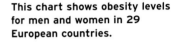

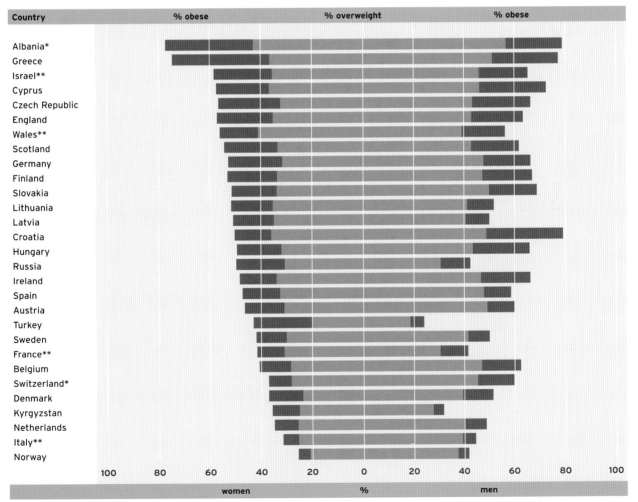

*Source:* International Obesity Task Force

* Urban   ** Self-reported

Australia, a country traditionally associated with sporting activities and the outdoor life, is also suffering from an obesity epidemic. With around seven million Australians already overweight or obese it is expected that 75 percent of the population will be overweight or obese by 2020.

Many parts of the developing world are now being affected by the obesity crisis too. In Africa obesity is on the rise amongst those who have moved to the cities, while those in rural areas continue to go hungry. Ghana, for example, now has as many overweight as underweight people.

**Increasing numbers of young people are overweight. These girls are at a special camp in the USA which aims to help them deal with their weight problem.**

## DEBATE

**You are in charge**

Your country is facing an obesity crisis. Half of the adult population is now obese and the health service cannot cope with the strain their obesity-linked illnesses are putting on the system. You are the government minister responsible for public health and have the following choices:

■ do nothing about obesity – it is not the government's responsibility to tell people how to live;

■ conduct a national obesity awareness and healthy eating campaign to inform people about the problem;

■ place a tax on foods that cause obesity to discourage people from buying them.

**What would you do?**

# CHAPTER 2

# What Causes Obesity?

**It's 2020 and a Saturday night in El Paso, Texas, in the USA.** Carlos and his family sit down in front of the television ready for their evening meal. Their favourite fast food restaurant has just delivered four 'two-for-the-price-of-one' king-sized meals. The family ordered them online through the television without even leaving their chairs.

Most of their shopping is done this way. In 2020 there is no need to go to a restaurant to pick up your takeaway unless you want to. There is also no need to go to a supermarket and walk around when you can order online and get someone else to do the shopping for you.

In the old days, people used to walk or ride their bikes into El Paso's town centre, but the town centre has virtually closed down because lots of out-of-town shopping malls have been built.

There are so many cars on the roads, it's not safe to cycle. None of the children are allowed to have bikes because it is too dangerous. Carlos is looking forward to getting his driving licence. In the USA in 2020 more than half the population is obese.

### A supersized issue

Although the reasons for gaining weight seem to be quite straightforward – a matter of taking in more energy than is actually used up – the actual causes of obesity are more complex. Food producers, advertising agencies, local and national governments, as well as the general public, have all played a part in the current obesity crisis.

### Too much food

In the 1970s the Western population was growing more slowly than the food supply. But instead of producing less food to match the needs of the smaller population, producers continued to grow and make more than was needed. This meant that those involved in the food industry would not lose money and jobs.

But what happened to the extra food? One solution was to make the existing population want to buy and eat more. The introduction of supersized portions and low prices – particularly in the USA – encouraged people to overeat.

Food is now available just about 24 hours a day in the developed world. It can be bought from supermarkets, fast food restaurants, takeaways and kiosks on the street. The way we eat has also changed. It is acceptable to eat anywhere – on the way to school or work, and on the way home after an evening out.

**Here is a list of well-known foods, their calorie content and the amount of activity required to burn them off.**

| Food | Nutritional content | | Minutes required to burn off by activity | | |
| --- | --- | --- | --- | --- | --- |
| | Calories | Fat grams | Walking slowly | Walking quickly | Strenuous activity |
| Mars bar (65g) | 294 | 11.4 | 98 | 59 | 39 |
| Popcorn (100g) | 405 | 7.7 | 135 | 81 | 54 |
| Big Mac (215g) | 492 | 23 | 164 | 98 | 66 |
| Cheeseburger | 379 | 18.9 | 126 | 76 | 51 |
| Kentucky Fried Chicken (67g) | 195 | 12 | 65 | 39 | 26 |
| Hamburger (108g) | 254 | 7.7 | 85 | 51 | 34 |
| Pizza deluxe (1 slice/66g) | 171 | 6.7 | 57 | 34 | 23 |
| Pizza (135g) | 263 | 4.9 | 88 | 53 | 35 |
| Potato wedges (135g) | 279 | 13 | 93 | 56 | 37 |
| Chicken tikka (150g) | 232 | 6.2 | 77 | 46 | 31 |
| Can of coke (330ml) | 139 | 0 | 46 | 28 | 19 |

Source: Obesity: Third Report of Session 2003-04 by the House of Commons Health Committee, 2004, page 134

## Modern life

Meals used to be prepared three times a day and were usually eaten at home. In the home environment, the cook had complete control over the amount of fat and sugar that went into meals. This control is no longer possible when much of what we eat is bought from restaurants or as ready-made meals from supermarkets.

In modern homes food is always available. Large appliances like fridges and freezers allow us to buy and store more food; microwaves allow it to be cooked more quickly. The days when someone would walk to the town centre or village and buy just enough food for a day or so and carry it home have long gone.

The type of food that is available has also changed. Government policies like the Common Agricultural Policy (CAP), which affects the European Union, make it more worthwhile and cheaper for farmers to produce greater amounts of sugar and dairy products rather than more fruit and vegetables.

Under the CAP, farmers are paid to produce extra sugar and dairy products. They are also paid to destroy any extra fruit and vegetables they grow rather than selling them more cheaply or even giving them away to people who can't afford them. The result is that food which is high in fat and sugar is cheaper to buy than healthy options.

Nowadays, people rarely eat three meals a day in their homes. Food is available to take away and eat just about anywhere.

## THE DIET OF CHILDREN AND ADULTS IN ENGLAND

**Overall, adults are eating:**
- More than twice the amount of saturated fat they need
- Half the fruit and vegetables needed
- Half the fibre needed
- Half the fish needed

**Overall, children are eating:**
- More than twice the amount of saturated fat they need
- A quarter of the fruit and vegetables they need
- More than twice the salt needed
- More than twice the sugar needed

Source: *Storing up problems: the medical case for a slimmer nation* from Royal College of Physicians, 2004, page 18.

## Snack or meal?

Chocolate bars and bags of crisps are thought of as 'snack foods' – something to eat and keep us going between meals if we get hungry. However, king-sized chocolate bars weighing 100 grams can contain as many as 400 calories. This is as many calories as a meal of lean grilled meat, potatoes and green vegetables weighing 400 grams.

A chocolate bar is 'energy dense'. This means it doesn't weigh very much, but contains a lot of calories. Because the bar weighs very little compared to a meal it doesn't create a lasting feeling of fullness and so the body feels it needs to eat something else soon.

Frequent snacking can easily lead to quick weight gain. Eating one chocolate bar, a packet of crisps and one fizzy drink per day can put someone nearly 800 calories over the recommended adult intake. Just 400 unused calories a day, stored every day for a year, can result in a weight gain of 18.6 kilograms!

## The power of advertising

Advertising on television, at cinemas, on the Internet and in magazines may also be responsible for the rise in obesity. Some countries, like Sweden, believe so strongly that advertising influences children that they have banned advertising from television during children's programmes. Companies producing snack foods spend large sums of money advertising their products. In 2002 in the UK, 178.2 million pounds was spent by companies advertising chocolate, sweets and crisps, whereas just 2.8 million pounds was spent advertising fresh fruit. The picture is similar in the USA where about 25 billion dollars is spent annually on food and drink advertising. Most of the

Unhealthy foods like ice creams and chocolates are advertised and available just about everywhere. Manufacturers spend millions of pounds promoting 'junk foods'.

advertising focuses upon highly packaged and processed food.

In contrast, government-backed healthy eating campaigns usually have much smaller advertising budgets. For example, the UK government's healthy eating 'five a day' campaign, promoting the need to eat five portions of fruit and vegetables every day to stay healthy, involved a relatively small advertising spend of five million pounds in 2002.

In 1997, the US Department of Agriculture spent 333 million dollars on nutrition education, evaluation and demonstrations – a relatively small amount in comparison with the billions spent by US companies on food and drink advertising.

As well as advertising, food companies promote their products in other ways too. 'On pack' offers involve collecting tokens on a package to get toys. Sometimes a toy will even be stuck to or inserted into a product to encourage people to buy it.

Fast food promotions which offer collectible toys to children as part of a meal may also be contributing to the obesity problem. One fast food chain, according to a UK government report, offered 98 toys to collect in a year. To collect every toy a child would have had to eat one high-calorie, high-fat fast food meal every 3.7 days. A standard-sized children's meal from a fast food restaurant containing one hamburger, an order of French fries and a fizzy drink contains about 600 calories and 20 grams of fat. The recommended intake for a normally active ten-year-old child is between 1,740 and 1,970 calories a day and 35 grams of fat.

## US FOOD MARKETING AND ADVERTISING EXPENDITURE, 1997-1998

| | |
|---|---|
| Breakfast cereals | 792 million dollars |
| Sweets and chocolate | 765 million dollars |
| Soft drinks | 549 million dollars |
| Snacks | 330 million dollars |

One fast-food hamburger chain spent 571 million dollars advertising their products in 1997-1998.

Source: http://youthxchange.e-meta.net/main/getyoursnack.asp

## Sitting targets

Inactivity also contributes to obesity. When we are not active, we burn off calories much more slowly – and modern life has made us more inactive than ever before. Watching television, which burns off very few calories, has had a large effect on our activity levels. The average hours of television watched per household per day in the US has increased from five hours and seven minutes per day in 1960 to eight hours per day in 2003.

Computer games have also affected activity levels. Children who are allowed to play them whenever and for as long as they like are less likely to run around and play outside.

We also walk less to get from A to B. The average person in the UK now walks 304.2 kilometres per year – 106.2 kilometres less than 25 years ago. Americans are also walking less. In the USA only 5.4 percent of trips are now made on foot, and cars are being used to drive very short distances. The number of walking journeys made by Americans for distances of less than a mile (1.6 km) has decreased by 42 per cent in 20 years.

New Zealand, traditionally associated with outdoor sports and walking, has noticed a similar decline. Trips made on foot dropped three percent to 400,000 a day between 1989 and 1998; a third of motor vehicle trips were for distances of less than two kilometres.

### DEBATE

**You are in charge**

As the head of a company that makes crisps, you have been accused of encouraging obesity with your products. You are worried that customers might stop buying your crisps if they think they will make them fat. You want to find some way of keeping your customers happy and stemming the tide of obesity.

What would you do?

Cycling used to be a popular way of getting around, but people are cycling less and less largely because of safety concerns. There are few cycle lanes and more cars. Twenty-three billion kilometres were cycled in the UK in 1952, but only four billion kilometres are cycled now. The sight of children cycling, playing outside and walking to school is also not as common as it used to be because parents are concerned about safety.

**Children who watch lots of television are less likely to play more active games outside and will gain weight because of their inactivity.**

## Other causes

Hereditary factors can also help to explain why some people gain weight more easily than others. Researchers have found that some families have slower metabolisms – their bodies burn up energy more slowly – which means they are more inclined to gain weight than families with faster metabolisms.

There are also psychological factors which make people overeat. Some people overeat because they are unhappy, bored or depressed. Food represents a form of comfort to them.

# CHAPTER 3

# Obesity and Health

**Peter's father is a doctor at a hospital in Munich, Germany.** He arrives home from work and looks at Peter in despair. 'Today we had such bad news. We can't afford any more kidney dialysis machines for the hospital. Our waiting lists are so long and I know that people – some of them children – are going to die before we can treat them. How can I face their parents? How can I do my job properly?'

It's May 2020. Peter is 12 years old. He is one of the lucky ones – his parents were determined that he would not become part of the obesity crisis that everyone was warned about at the beginning of the century. Peter's diet has been healthy and the family makes sure he gets the government-recommended hour of exercise every day. But Peter's family is rare. In his area more than 30 percent of children under 12 are obese diabetics. Some of them need dialysis – treatment to rid the blood of toxins – because their condition is so bad. When the kidneys fail, treatment must be given within three months or the patient will die.

## Health problems

Obesity increases the chances of people suffering from serious and potentially lethal diseases. These can include heart disease, Type 2 diabetes and different types of cancer. Because of these and other health problems, someone who is obese is expected to live nine years less than a person of normal weight.

## What is diabetes?

Diabetes develops when the body can't use glucose (sugar) properly. This can be because there isn't enough of the hormone insulin in the body or because the insulin available simply doesn't work properly. Insulin is made and stored in an organ called the pancreas.

There are two types of diabetes – Type 1 and Type 2. In Type 1 diabetes, the body is unable to produce any insulin. This type of diabetes usually starts in childhood or young adulthood. It's treated with diet control and insulin injections. Type 1 diabetes used to be called 'insulin-dependent diabetes' or 'juvenile diabetes'.

In Type 2 diabetes the pancreas may not produce enough insulin, or the insulin that is produced doesn't work properly. This tends to affect people as they get older, and usually appears after the age of 40. It used to be known as 'maturity-onset diabetes' or 'non-insulin-dependent diabetes'.

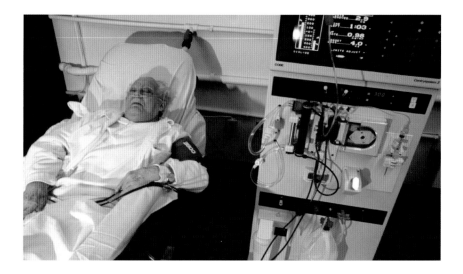

**A patient undergoing kidney dialysis. Obesity can cause Type 2 diabetes, which may lead to kidney failure. Dialysis is then needed to do the kidneys' job of eliminating toxins from the blood.**

As well as being associated with middle age, Type 2 diabetes is also associated with being overweight or obese and is on the rise amongst obese children and young adults. The American Diabetic Association has predicted that one in three American children born in 2000 will become diabetic in their lifetime.

**This chart shows how those with above-average body mass indexes are more prone to certain medical conditions.**

| Prevalence of medical conditions by Body Mass Index | | | | | | | | |
|---|---|---|---|---|---|---|---|---|
| Medical condition | Men Body Mass Index | | | | Women Body Mass Index | | | |
| | 8.5 to 24.9 | 25 to 29.9 | 30 to 34.9 | over 40 | 8.5 to 24.9 | 25 to 29.9 | 30 to 34.9 | over 40 |
| Type 2 diabetes | 2.03 | 4.93 | 10.1 | 10.65 | 2.38 | 7.12 | 7.24 | 19.89 |
| Coronary heart disease | 8.84 | 9.6 | 16.01 | 13.97 | 6.87 | 11.13 | 12.56 | 19.22 |
| High blood pressure | 23.47 | 34.16 | 48.95 | 64.53 | 23.26 | 38.77 | 47.95 | 63.16 |
| Osteoarthritis | 2.59 | 4.55 | 4.66 | 10.04 | 5.22 | 8.51 | 9.94 | 17.19 |
| Prevalence ratio (%) | | | | | | | | |

*Source: American Obesity Association / NHANES III, 1988-1994*

**The effects of diabetes**

Diabetes can be treated in several ways. Sufferers may be given insulin injections, insulin pills, a special diet, or combinations of any of these treatments.

If diabetes is not treated it can cause heart disease, stroke, blindness and kidney failure. Diabetes can also damage the nerves, making people less aware of pressure or injury to parts of their body. This can lead to leg ulcers and if these do not respond to treatment, doctors may have to amputate a patient's limbs.

One of the biggest worries about diabetes is the way it can affect the kidneys' ability to do their job. Over time, the high levels of sugar in the blood caused by diabetes can damage the millions of tiny filtering units within each kidney.

The kidneys' function is to cleanse the blood of toxins and transform waste in the body into urine. The body's two kidneys can get rid of about three litres of urine per day. When they don't work properly, harmful salts and fluids build up in the body, and then dialysis – removing the toxins from the blood with a machine – can be necessary.

Treatment of kidney failure currently costs the UK's National Health Service two billion pounds each year. In the USA, kidney dialysis and renal transplants cost more than 35 billion dollars annually.

**Heart problems**

If someone is overweight or obese they need more oxygen and so their body has to create more blood. The heart then has to work

## CANCER

Certain types of cancer are linked with obesity. In men and women obesity is associated with cancers of the oesophagus, colon, rectum, liver, gall bladder, pancreas and kidneys. Obese women may also suffer from cancers of the breast, uterus and cervix. Obese men have a higher chance of getting stomach and prostate cancer.

harder to pump the blood around; this in turn puts such a strain on the heart that it can damage it and cause high blood pressure.

Obesity is also linked with heart disease. Heart disease is a build-up of fatty materials within the walls of the arteries – this is called atherosclerosis. These fatty materials narrow the arteries and reduce the space through which blood can flow. They may also block the delivery of nutrients to the artery walls, causing them to lose their elasticity. The blood therefore finds it harder to move around and carry the oxygen that the body needs to survive. Heart disease also means that the blood is more inclined to clot which can lead to a life-threatening condition called thrombosis and make heart attacks more likely.

People with heart disease can experience a feeling of heaviness, tightness or pain in the middle of their chest that can affect the rest of their upper body too. Running, playing sports or even going upstairs can bring the symptoms on. They may feel constantly tired.

An artery, highly magnified, clogged up with fat. Heart disease is caused by a build up of fat within the arteries which makes it more difficult for blood to move through the body.

Heart disease can be treated by drugs. However, if the arteries are badly blocked, the drugs may not work and surgery may be needed to open up or replace the arteries.

### Osteoarthritis

Extra weight places an increased strain on the body's joints and this in turn can lead to osteoarthritis, a disease affecting the body's joints. This joint disorder can become very disabling and painful.

### Psychological problems

Sadly, obese people are often depressed because they feel bad about themselves and are sometimes treated badly by others. Obese women are around 37 percent more likely to commit suicide than women of a healthy weight.

Obesity can make people feel very badly about themselves; they may even suffer from depression.

### Counting the cost

The health problems caused by obesity are already affecting people's ability to do their jobs. In the USA, for example, 130 million adults are overweight or obese and this costs an estimated 117 billion dollars in medical expenses and lost productivity. Severely obese Americans are 60 percent more expensive to treat than Americans of normal weight.

Obesity costs the UK's National Health Service 500 million pounds per year in terms of treatment. The wider cost to industry in terms of lost working days brings the total cost to more than two billion pounds. The Australian government estimate that obesity is costing their country 1.5 billion dollars per year in direct health costs.

If obesity continues to rise among young people, the medical and economic costs will also continue to grow. This may lead to tax rises in countries with a government-funded health care service. In countries without a health care service, medical costs will rise, and obese people risk becoming impoverished and even dying because they cannot afford treatment.

**Estimates of the direct costs of obesity**

| Country | Year of estimate | Proportion of total healthcare expenditure due to obesity | Prevalance of obesity (BMI over 30) | |
| | | | At time of estimate (%) | 2003 (%) |
| --- | --- | --- | --- | --- |
| USA | 2000 | 4.8 | 30.5 | 30.5 |
| Netherlands | 1981-89 | 4.0 | 5.0 | 10.3 |
| Canada | 1997 | 2.4 | 14.0 | 13.9 |
| Portugal | 1996 | 3.5 | 11.5 | 14.0 |
| Australia | 1989-90 | more than 2.0 | 10.8 | 22.0 |
| England | 1998 | 1.5 | 19.0 | 23.5 |
| France | 1992 | 1.5 | 6.5 | 9.0 |

*Source: Obesity: Third Report of Session 2003-04 by the House of Commons Health Committee, 2004, page 123*

## Treating adult obesity

Obese adults need specialist medical treatment. This may involve a weight loss programme, nutritional education, counselling and sometimes the use of drugs to suppress appetites or drugs that can affect the way the body absorbs fat. Surgery may also be used to reduce the size of an obese person's stomach so that they feel full after eating a small amount.

This table shows estimates of how much has been spent on treating obesity-related illnesses as a proportion of total spending on health across a range of countries. It also shows how the obesity rate has changed in those countries since the estimates were made.

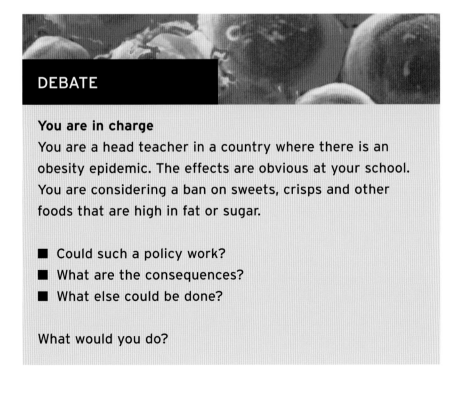

## DEBATE

**You are in charge**
You are a head teacher in a country where there is an obesity epidemic. The effects are obvious at your school. You are considering a ban on sweets, crisps and other foods that are high in fat or sugar.

- Could such a policy work?
- What are the consequences?
- What else could be done?

What would you do?

# CHAPTER 4

# Obesity in Children and Young People

**Alice is 17 and a school council president in New York State, USA, in 2020.** She sits at the school board meeting and listens to the problems her school faces. The buildings are in a poor state of repair and there is no money to fix them. Education has received less government funding in recent years; taxes have been put up to cope with medical costs caused by the USA's growing obesity crisis.

More than half the students in Alice's school are severely overweight. The school is in a poor area; there are few opportunities for keeping fit and even the local swimming pool is too expensive for most people. Many of the children in the area have joint problems because they are so heavy and they find it hard to walk even short distances without getting out of breath.

Today, Alice, the school board and the principal must decide whether to accept an offer to sell off the last school athletics field to a developer who wants to build a shopping mall. They know the money can be used to repair the school buildings, but they also know school is the only place that some children get any exercise at all. Without this athletics field the health of the students will be badly affected...

### A growing problem

Although most obese or overweight children do not have serious health problems while they are young, they are very likely to suffer health problems if they remain obese as they grow up.

Researchers have found that overweight young people have a greater chance of being overweight adults and that weight problems seem to run in families. The American Obesity Association reports that overweight children aged from 10 to 14 with at least one overweight or obese parent have a 79 percent chance of being overweight adults.

Like adults, young people will start to gain weight if the amount of energy taken in is more than the amount they burn off. The unused energy is turned into fat cells and the fat cells continue to be produced until the end of puberty.

Poor dietary habits, lack of activity and the resulting weight gain can affect whole families.

## DEFINING CHILDHOOD OBESITY

Definitions for childhood obesity vary from country to country, but recent guidelines from the US Centers for Disease Control (CDC) state that the term *obese* should not be used for children at all. The centre uses the terms *overweight* and *at risk for overweight*. An overweight child is defined as one who has a BMI higher than the BMIs for 95 per cent of all children their age. A child who is at risk for overweight is one who has a BMI higher than the BMIs for 85 per cent, but not higher than the BMIs for 95 per cent, of all children their age.

In this book, the term *overweight*, when used to describe children, is equivalent to the CDC term *at risk for overweight*, and the term *obese* when referring to children is equivalent to the CDC term *overweight*.

## Fat programming

During puberty, the sex hormones – oestrogen for girls, and testosterone for boys – are triggered. These hormones define the areas in which the fat cells grow. Once the fat cells are established, when puberty ends, these cells can get bigger or smaller depending on the amount of fat in them. There is nothing anyone can do to get rid of the fat cells – they can only burn up the fat within them.

Because of the large number of fat cells within their bodies it is difficult for people who were obese as children to lose weight when they are older. It is as though the body has been programmed to be overweight. Obese and overweight children can have up to three times as many fat cells in their bodies as children of normal weight.

## The scale of the issue

Many doctors and scientists believe that obesity amongst children is a serious issue which is likely to get worse if action is not taken. The World Health Organization has estimated that 3.3 percent of the world's pre-school children are now overweight. The number of

A food pyramid showing the recommended proportions of different types of food needed for a healthy diet. The foods shown at the top should only be eaten in small quantities.

obese children in the UK has tripled in 20 years. Ten percent of 6-year-olds are obese, as are 17 percent of 15-year-olds.

In the USA, 30.3 percent of children aged 6 to 11 are overweight, and 15 percent within this age range are obese. In the case of American adolescents, 30.4 percent of young people aged 12 to 19 are overweight and 15 percent are obese.

## Treating childhood obesity

In adults, the body mass index (BMI) is used as an indicator of obesity. The BMI is also applied in the case of children, but it is used alongside other growth charts which take into account a child's rate of growth, their height, their sex and their age.

Many experts believe that it is not a good idea for most overweight children to be put on a weight loss plan, as this could affect their growth. Placing overweight children on strict diets can make them feel badly about themselves. This low self esteem can then lead to anorexia nervosa, a psychological illness which makes people eat increasingly less until they severely damage their health and sometimes even die.

Overweight children are usually encouraged to maintain their weight – not gain any more – with the expectation that as they get taller they will grow into it. They are also advised to take part in more physical activity. Walking, swimming, cycling, aerobics and

| Age | Males (calories) | Females (calories) |
|---|---|---|
| 0-3 months | 545 | 515 |
| 4-6 months | 690 | 645 |
| 7-9 months | 825 | 765 |
| 10-12 months | 920 | 865 |
| 1-3 years | 1,230 | 1,165 |
| 4-6 years | 1,715 | 1,545 |
| 7-10 years | 1,970 | 1,740 |
| 11-14 years | 2,220 | 1,845 |
| 15-18 years | 2,755 | 2,110 |
| 19-50 years | 2,550 | 1,940 |
| 51-59 years | 2,550 | 1,900 |
| 60-64 years | 2,380 | 1,900 |
| 65-74 years | 2,330 | 1,900 |
| over 74 years | 2,100 | 1,810 |

This chart shows the average estimated energy requirements for people of different ages.

Source: Obesity: Third Report of Session 2003-04 by the House of Commons Health Committee, 2004, page 132

other sports can all help to stop further weight gain. British and American government guidelines state that children need at least one hour of physical activity per day to stay healthy.

Obese children need specialist treatment and care. They may be put on a weight loss programme and given counselling. In some countries extremely obese children may be given an operation to reduce the size of their stomach so that they feel full after eating a small amount of food. Although there are drugs available to treat adult obesity, none of these are currently recommended for children under sixteen.

The most effective prescription for overweight children is to change their eating habits (cutting out junk foods); adopt a healthy, well-balanced diet; and engage in more physical activity.

Obesity in children is a more serious matter and specialist help from doctors, dietitians and counsellors is usually recommended for them and their families. In adults, obesity can be treated with drugs that suppress the appetite, and surgery that makes the stomach smaller so it cannot hold so much food, but these practices are not usually recommended for children.

## The causes of obesity in children

Scientists believe there are a variety of factors which contribute to obesity in young people.

*Genetic inheritance*  Scientists have found some evidence that in a small number of cases obesity can be inherited. Researchers have identified families that have lower metabolic rates. A slow metabolism means that the body doesn't burn off energy so quickly and makes it easier to gain weight.

Scientists have also found that some genes can increase or decrease appetites. This has the effect of making some people more

| Period | Percentage of US children (aged 6 to 11) who are obese | | Percentage of US adolescents (aged 12 to 19) who are obese | |
|---|---|---|---|---|
| | Boys | Girls | Boys | Girls |
| 1999-2000 | 16 | 14.5 | 15.5 | 15.5 |
| 1988-1994 | 11.6 | 11 | 11.3 | 9.7 |
| 1971-1974 | 4.3 | 3.6 | 6.1 | 6.2 |

The following chart shows how obesity has increased among American children since 1974.

Source: *Obesity*: CDC, National Center for Health Statistics, National Health and Nutrition Examination Survey. Ogden *et al.* JAMA. 2002;288:1728-1732.

hungry than others or making them feel they have to eat a lot before they feel full. As a result, those with genes that cause increased appetites have a tendency to overeat and gain weight. Furthermore, there is some evidence that genes can influence food preferences. These genes may determine whether people naturally choose to eat sweet or savoury foods.

*Birth weight* Studies have suggested that a person is more likely to become obese later in life if they have a low birth weight, because they did not get the nourishment they needed when they were developing in the womb. The evidence for this is much stronger than evidence linking a high birth weight to obesity in later life.

*Breastfeeding* Research has also shown that breastfed babies may be less at risk of becoming obese. In Scotland, scientists studied 32,000

**A shopping trolley full of unhealthy, highly processed food. Most experts recommend that a healthy diet should include at least five portions of fruit and vegetables per day.**

children and found obesity was 30 percent less common among those who had been breastfed as babies. A team at the Cincinnati Children's Hospital Medical Center in the USA found high levels of a protein that affects the body's processing of fat, in breastmilk. Feeding babies breastmilk for the first 6 to 12 months of their lives is believed by many scientists to be the best way to prevent obesity in children.

*Overeating* Children who take in more calories than they burn off are likely to become overweight or obese. High-fat foods contain more calories and are, as a result, harder to burn off.

*Inactivity* If a person is inactive then the calories they take in will not be burned off. Children who do not take part in physical activities, but prefer to watch television or play computer games are more likely to gain weight. Some research has linked obesity directly with television viewing, reporting that the more television someone watches the fatter they become.

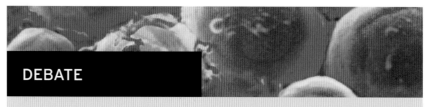

## DEBATE

**You are in charge**
You are a parent. How would you encourage your obese children to watch less television, take more exercise and eat properly? Who do you believe is responsible for childhood obesity?

- Parents?
- The government?
- Food producers?
- Advertising agencies?

Should advertisements for unhealthy foods be banned? What would you do?

*Social and economic factors* Some research shows that people in deprived areas who have not had a good education are more likely to become obese. High-fat, high-sugar foods like crisps and cakes are cheaper for many families than healthy alternatives like fresh fruit and vegetables.

### Effects on health

Obesity in children can lead to various health problems, including the development of Type 2 diabetes. High blood pressure is nine times more common in obese children than in non-obese. Obese children can also suffer from orthopaedic complaints such as overgrowing and bowing of the leg bones.

Some obese children and adults suffer from snoring and sleep apnoea – disordered breathing – as they try to sleep. Too much fat in the chest wall and abdomen makes it harder to breathe normally, and the capacity of the lungs is actually reduced. Fat also collects around the upper airway – particularly the larynx – which may stop the air going through these passages at night when someone is lying down.

### Psychological problems

Sadly, obese and overweight children can also suffer psychological problems because of their size. Many report that they are teased and bullied about their weight at school and that friends, family and even strangers can make hurtful comments.

As a result, it is quite common for obese young people to feel very negative about themselves. Some suffer from depression. Others eat even more to try to make themselves feel better, or they may not want to go out in case they are bullied.

**Sometimes obese children are bullied at school. This can make them suffer from low self esteem and want to eat even more to try to make themselves feel better.**

# CHAPTER 5

# Obesity in the Developing World

**Sanjeev takes off his school uniform for the last time.** He is 13 years old and tomorrow he starts work breaking up stones in the local quarry. There, with his three brothers, he will work from dawn to dusk for just a few rupees a day.

Once Sanjeev thought he would be a doctor, but this is no longer possible. There is no longer any money to send him to school; all of his brothers and sisters need to work now to keep their father alive.

Sanjeev's father was once the well-to-do manager of a computer call centre. But like many people with well-paid jobs in India he ate too much, gained too much weight and then diabetes set in. He is now almost blind and too ill to work; he depends on his family to pay for the insulin injections that he needs several times a day.

The year is 2020 and there are families like this in cities all over India. In the old days, people in India never seemed to have enough food to eat. This is still the case in some rural areas, but in the cities many people are overweight or obese and there is not enough money to pay for their treatment. India now has the highest rate of diabetes in the world.

### A worldwide epidemic

Obesity is usually seen as a health issue that affects those who live in developed nations such as the USA and the UK.

However, recent research shows that obesity is a problem that is spreading outside the West. The World Health Organization estimates that there are 300 million obese adults in the world and 115 million of them live in developing countries.

Not all developing countries keep statistics on obesity, but the statistics that are available show a growing problem that experts believe should be watched carefully. They are concerned that the rising obesity rate could cause developing countries to plunge further into debt as they try to fight hunger on one hand and obesity on the other.

Africa, so often associated with starvation and famine, has a high incidence of obesity in some areas. In Zambia, nearly 20 percent of the adult population is obese, as are 25 percent of Egyptian adults.

In the Cape Peninsula of South Africa, 44 percent of adult women suffer from obesity, while Ghana has as many overweight as underweight people. In sub-Saharan Africa, where most of the world's hungry live, there is an increase in obesity amongst educated women living in the cities.

**Although many people in Africa do not have enough food to eat, obesity is on the rise in some African towns and cities.**

## DIABETES

One of the most serious obesity-related diseases in the developing world is diabetes. India, for example, now has the world's largest diabetic population, with over 32 million people affected. Approximately 85 percent of these are suffering from Type 2 diabetes, and 90 percent of Type 2 diabetics are obese or overweight. The number of diabetics in India is expected to more than double by 2025.

By that year, the majority of people with diabetes in the developing world will be in the 45–64 age group; diabetes is the leading cause of blindness in people aged between 20 and 74. A low-income Indian family with an adult with diabetes may have to pay 25 percent of the family income towards diabetes care.

A meeting of Samoan chiefs. More than 79 percent of Samoan men living in urban areas are now obese.

## FEAST OR FAMINE?

- More than eight percent of children in North Africa are overweight, while seven percent are starving.
- In Eastern Asia, 4.3 percent of pre-school children are overweight and 3.4 percent are starving.
- Some countries, including Egypt, Malawi, Nigeria and Qatar, have a higher percentage of obese children than the USA.

Other available statistics from around the developing world are equally worrying.

Thirty percent of Chile's adult population are obese; Thai children are showing a rise in obesity, and in Samoa, 79 percent of men living in cities are obese. In China, the number of overweight people increased from 10 to 15 percent in three years. In Brazil and Colombia the proportion of overweight people is about 40 percent, which is similar to the proportion of overweight people in European countries.

## An urban cause

Many researchers believe that this rise in obesity, which occurs mainly in the cities of developing countries, has been caused by people adopting Western lifestyles as they move from rural areas to the cities.

Life in the rural areas of developing countries involves plenty of physical labour, including farming, collecting wood, carrying water and walking from place to place. In the cities, however, there is a rise in car ownership. People are walking less and taking either cars or buses to work. Many city dwellers work in offices and have a generally less active lifestyle than people who live in rural areas.

**This chart shows the percentage of women who are overweight in various parts of the developing world.**

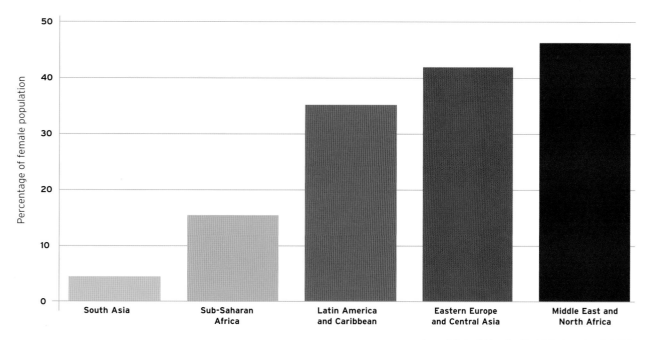

*Source:* R. Martorell, International Food Policy Research Institute, 2001.

The diet of those living in cities is different too. A traditional African rural diet is based on roots, tubers and coarse grains. In the cities, however, people are eating Western-style high-sugar, high-fat, processed foods and drinks. It is also easy to buy and eat food outside the home. Street vendors and food stalls are open seven days a week and until late at night, and food is almost as constantly available as it is in developed nations.

Although city dwellers are becoming heavier than their rural counterparts, they are also likely to suffer from malnutrition. They can suffer from iron deficiency and anaemia, as well as Vitamin A deficiency, which can cause blindness in children aged under five. This is because larger quantities of cheap food fill the stomach but may not give the body important vitamins and minerals.

## The effects of a modern lifestyle

The Pima Indians of Arizona are an example of a native people who have switched from a traditional diet to a Western, urban diet. Arizona Pimas have diets made up of about 40 percent fat and they do an average of about two hours of physical activity per week. By contrast, Pima Indians living in Mexico follow an active lifestyle that involves 23 hours of physical work per week and a traditional, low-fat diet. Arizona Pimas have a high incidence of obesity and Type 2

**This table shows how the effects of modernization - inactivity and a change of diet - can cause obesity in urban areas of developing countries.**

| Location or type of activity | Effect of modernization | Impact on obesity |
|---|---|---|
| Transportation | Rise in car ownership. Decrease in walking or cycling. | Increase in driving shorter distances. |
| At home | Increase in the use of modern appliances (e.g. microwaves, dishwashers, washing machines, vacuum cleaners). | Decrease in manual labour. |
| | Increase in ready-made foods and ingredients for cooking. | Increase in consumption of convenience foods that contribute to obesity. |
| | Increase in television viewing and computer and video game use. | Decrease in time spent on more active, recreational pursuits. |
| In the workplace | Increase in sedentary (tending to sit down a lot) lifestyles due to technology, especially the increase in computerization. | Decrease in physically demanding manual labour. |
| Public places | Increase in the use of elevators, escalators and automatic doors. | Decrease in daily physical activity patterns such as climbing stairs. |
| Living in the city | Increase in crime in urban areas. | Prevents women, children and the elderly from going out alone for exercise and leisure activities. |

*Source:* American Obesity Association

diabetes compared with Mexican Pimas. Studies of the Pimas have helped scientists learn more about the causes and effects of obesity.

## Counting the cost

The governments of developing countries are currently engaged in fighting a range of health problems including malnutrition and diseases such as typhoid, malaria and cholera. The health problems associated with rising obesity have the potential to create a further burden on their already overstretched medical resources.

However, despite the rise in obesity, hunger is still considered the biggest problem in the developing world. United Nations figures estimate that of the world's 815 million hungry people, 780 million live in developing countries.

A Pima Indian from Arizona being tested in water for his percentage of body fat.

## DEBATE

### You are in charge

You are a government minister in a developing country. What steps can you take to combat the growing problem of obesity in your country? How do the problems you face compare with those faced by governments in Western countries?

You are also one of the world's biggest producers of sugar cane. You would like to make sure that the sugar cane industry and its workers are on your side in the fight against obesity.

What would you do?

# CHAPTER 6

# Creating a Healthy Future

**At the United Nations Youth Summit in 2020**, young people from around the world are describing how the current obesity crisis affects their lives. Kyle, an 18-year-old American delegate, is angry. He blames governments, food producers and retailers for encouraging a culture of overeating that is destroying the health of millions of people.

Kyle speaks from experience. His father died from heart disease last year and the family is suing a fast food chain, demanding compensation for his death. Kyle believes that his father's life was shortened due to years of eating the chain's high-fat, high-salt food.

This legal action mirrors cases in the 1990s when families of smokers successfully sued tobacco companies for causing cancer in their loved ones. Kyle knows that the compensation will not bring his father back, but he wants to make the fast food chain take responsibility and, at the same time, draw attention to the plight of millions of other families in similar situations all around the world.

## Turning the tide

Individuals cannot stop the obesity crisis by themselves. Because it is a complex problem, the solutions need action and commitment from people working together in many different areas. Governments, educators, health professionals, food producers and retailers all need to cooperate to turn back the rising tide of obesity. National and local governments are able to create laws and pursue policies that can affect the health of a nation.

Laws can also be enacted to encourage people to take more exercise. For example, builders of roads, housing estates, shopping centres and office buildings could be required to provide good pedestrian access and safe cycle lanes. New buildings could be designed so that lifts and escalators are second choice to staircases

To try to stop the rise in obesity amongst their workers, some companies, like this one in Japan, have introduced fitness classes during working time.

wherever possible. Local governments could ensure that cheap and accessible leisure centres and parks with exercise facilities are provided for all.

Governments can also provide incentives to make it worthwhile for farmers to produce more fruit and vegetables. Currently, such incentives are rarely provided and many policies seem to work against a nation's health. American agricultural policy, like the European Common Agricultural Policy (CAP), can be considered an example of this. Since the 1930s, American farmers have received subsidies to produce crops like wheat, soybeans and corn. These subsidies were devised to keep American farmers in work and to provide enough food for the nation. However, there is now little financial incentive for farmers to produce fruits, vegetables and other grains.

This graph compares rates of coronary heart disease with fruit and vegetable consumption among men aged 35-74, across eleven European countries. It shows that the higher the consumption of fruit and vegetables in a particular country, the lower the death rate from heart disease.

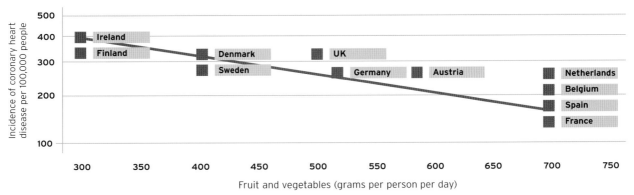

Source: Food and Agriculture Organization

Although corn, or maize, may be a healthy vegetable, it is turned into a high-calorie, commonly used sweetener called high-fructose corn syrup (HFCS). Similarly, soybeans, which are nutritious, are turned into fats that are used in cheap and unhealthy foods. By switching subsidies from these crops to fruit and vegetables, governments could make a big difference in the battle against obesity.

Governments can also place restrictions on the promotion and advertising of unhealthy food. In some parts of the world, governments have banned the television advertising of junk food to children. In Norway, television advertisements cannot be shown at times when programmes aimed at children under 12 are broadcast, and the province of Quebec in Canada has banned advertising aimed at children under 13. Placing a tax on unhealthy food to discourage people from buying it – in much the same way as alcohol and cigarettes are taxed – is another option.

**Education for change**

Education plays a vital role in encouraging children to lead healthier lifestyles. Obesity levels could be reduced by the introduction of healthy school meals, fruit tuck shops and vending machines, freely available drinking water, breakfast clubs and a range of different fitness activities designed to appeal to all children.

**School exercise and activity programmes, like this one in Schenectady, New York, are an important way of helping young people become fit and healthy.**

Some countries have already taken steps in this direction. In Scotland, water and fruit juice must be provided in school vending machines, and advertisements on the machines promoting sugary drinks and unhealthy snacks are banned. England offers a National School Fruit Scheme which offers every child aged four to six a free piece of fruit each day.

Singapore introduced a ten-year Trim and Fit Scheme in 1992 which involved training teachers in healthy eating and activities, reducing sugar in children's drinks and increasing physical activity for children during school hours. The scheme was successful in improving children's fitness, and led to a reduction in the national level of childhood obesity.

## SINGAPORE SUCCESS STORY

In 1992, Singapore government research found that 14 percent of the country's schoolchildren were obese. The Trim and Fit Scheme was introduced to reduce the levels of overweight and obese children in Singapore. Under the scheme, overweight and obese children participated in 1.5 hours of exercise a week in addition to weekly physical education sessions. Nutritional counselling was provided. Schools were given guidelines for the types of food that could be sold on the premises. By 2002, obesity levels among children in Singapore were reduced to 9.8 percent.

**Healthy schools**

Education about healthy lifestyles and how to choose and prepare healthy food could also be introduced into school curriculums. Nutrition experts believe that the trend towards convenience foods – which simply have to be heated up and eaten – has meant that cooking skills have been lost.

Young people can also be empowered to make decisions regarding healthy choices in their lives. Lessons about citizenship and personal, social and health education, as well as school policies that encourage positive decision making, can help them to achieve this.

By working closely with health care centres, health professionals and parents, schools can also provide support for young people who are overweight or obese, helping them to change their eating habits and take more exercise. Schools could also act to prevent overweight or obese children being bullied by their classmates.

## Health service in crisis

If nothing is done to halt the current dramatic rise in obesity rates, health services throughout the world are likely to become severely overstretched. To prevent this from happening, doctors, nurses and other health professionals need to be trained and given funding to spread healthy eating and healthy lifestyle messages throughout their

**If food packaging is labelled correctly, including the percentages of fat, sugar and salt the food contains, it is easier for people to make healthy choices.**

communities. Areas with high numbers of overweight and obese people would need more help and funding.

## Selling and producing food

Food retailers and supermarkets have an essential role to play in halting the obesity crisis. They can stock a wider range of healthy foods, and offer them at prices that poorer customers can afford. They can also encourage shoppers to buy them through healthy eating campaigns. By removing sweets and crisps from the checkout areas, supermarkets can reduce their customers' exposure to unhealthy choices.

The battle against obesity can also be helped by clearer and more accurate food labelling. People frequently do not appreciate what is in the food they buy, because the labels are not easily understandable. Laws could be passed to ensure that labels present the product's nutritional content in a way that is easily understood, and not misleading. For example, the phrase '85 percent fat free' does not clearly say that the product actually contains 15 percent fat. Similarly, a product that is labelled 'fat free' could still be high in sugar.

## North Karelia project

An example of how a government can work with health professionals, teachers, food producers and retailers to improve the health of a community is the North Karelia project in Finland. In the

This chart shows the improvements in the coronary heart disease mortality rate among men aged 35-64 in North Karelia and Finland as a result of the North Karelia project.

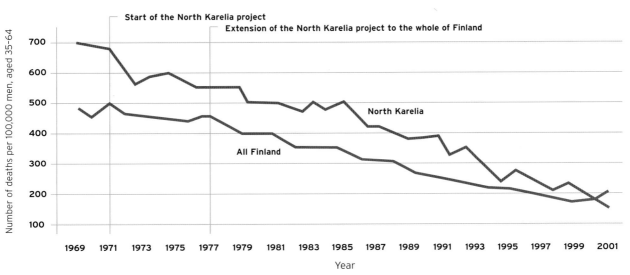

*Source: Heart views*

1960s, Finnish men had the highest death rate from heart disease in the world. North Karelia, in the east of the country, was a particular black spot. In 1972 the Finnish government, working with the World Health Organization, stepped in to help.

The problem was found to be the North Karelian diet. North Karelia is a dairy farming area and consequently the local people ate lots of high-fat dairy products such as butter, cream, whole milk and cheese. Few fruits and vegetables were consumed; in fact, many in the farming community felt that green vegetables should only be eaten by cattle.

Doctors, nurses, teachers, social workers and counsellors were all trained to help the North Karelians adopt a more healthy lifestyle. Healthy eating practices were introduced at workplaces and schools; competitions were held to encourage people to lose weight with the help of nutrition experts; supermarkets were urged to promote the sale of fruit and vegetables. The farmers were also encouraged to grow crops of berries, which grow well in Finland, to supply the fruit that was so desperately needed in their diets.

So encouraging were the early results that in 1977, the project was extended to the whole of Finland. The North Karelia project ended in 1997. It had been a spectacular success, with the number of deaths from coronary heart disease having dropped by 82 percent. Life expectancy among men rose by eight years, from 65 to 73.

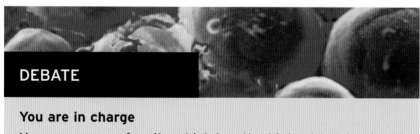

**DEBATE**

**You are in charge**
You are mayor of a city which has the highest levels of obesity in the whole country.
You want to start up an equivalent of the North Karelia project. How are you going to plan the campaign? Who would you need to work with?

**What would you do?**

The consumption of fruit and vegetables climbed from the lowest in Europe to the highest in northern Europe. The project led to dietary changes throughout Finland. Between 1969 and 2002, deaths from chronic heart disease dropped by 76 percent among Finnish men aged 35 to 64.

Today, the North Karelia project is used by the World Health Organization as an effective model for improving the health of communities. The WHO has set up similar projects in other countries and regions, including China, South and North America and the Middle East.

**Patients being weighed at a fat reduction hospital in China. The hospital aims to help people lose weight through a combination of diet, exercise and acupuncture.**

# Glossary

**anaemia** A condition in which someone does not have enough red blood cells, or their red blood cells do not contain enough haemoglobin (a protein containing iron), resulting in poor health.

**anorexia nervosa** A life-threatening eating disorder in which someone is obsessed by losing weight, causing them to diet excessively.

**Body Mass Index (BMI)** A person's weight in kilograms divided by their height in metres squared. The BMI is used to show whether someone is underweight, a normal weight, overweight or obese.

**calorie** A unit used to measure the energy contained within food and used by our bodies.

**Common Agricultural Policy (CAP)** A policy of the European Union that determines what can be farmed within the EU and what farmers can be paid for their produce.

**dialysis** A treatment that filters the waste products from the blood of patients whose kidneys are not functioning properly. It is carried out by a kidney dialysis machine.

**energy dense** Describes certain foods such as crisps and chocolate bars that contain lots of calories for their weight.

**insulin** A hormone created by the pancreas that regulates the level of sugar in the blood.

**iron deficiency** Inadequate iron in the body. This can lead to anaemia when someone does not have enough red blood cells. Iron can be obtained from meat and green leafy vegetables.

**metabolism** The process by which a body absorbs food and converts it into energy.

**oestrogen** A female sex hormone.

**osteoarthritis** A disease affecting the body's joints.

**testosterone** A male sex hormone.

**vitamin A** Also known as *retinol*, vitamin A is found in vegetables, egg yolk and fish liver oil and is essential for growth.

# Further Information

## Websites

BBC Online
www.bbc.co.uk/health/

American Obesity Association
www.obesity.org

Better health channel Australia
www.betterhealth.vic.gov.au

International Food Policy Research Institute
www.ifpri.org

World Health Organization
http://www.who.int/en/

Food and Agriculture Organization of the United Nations
www.fao.org

British Nutrition Foundation
www.nutrition.org.uk

Food Standards Agency
www.foodstandards.gov.uk/healthiereating

Diabetes UK
www.diabetes.org.uk/home.htm

American Diabetes Association
http://www.diabetes.org/home.jsp

National Obesity Forum
www.nationalobesityforum.org.uk/

World Diabetes Foundation
www.worlddiabetesfoundation.org

## Books

### Non-Fiction

*Fat Land: How Americans Became the Fattest People in the World* by Greg Critser (Penguin Books, 2004)

*Our Overweight Children: What Parents, Schools and Communities can do to Control the Fatness Epidemic* by Sharon Dalton (University of California Press, 2004)

*Obesity: Third Report of Session* 2003–04 by the House of Commons Health Committee (The Stationery Office, 2004)

*Not on the Label: What Really Goes into the Food on Your Plate* by Felicity Lawrence (Penguin Books, 2004)

*Storing up problems: the medical case for a slimmer nation* (Royal College of Physicians, 2004)

*Fast Food Nation: What the All-American Meal is Doing to the World* by Eric Schlosser (Penguin Books, 2002)

*Fueling the Teen Machine* by Ellen Shanley and Colleen Thompson (Bull Publishing, 2001)

### Fiction

*Fat Boy Swim* by Catherine Forde (Egmont Books, 2003)

*The Fat Man* by Maurice Gee (Puffin, 2001)

*Fat Kid Rules the World* by K. L. Going (Corgi, 2004)

# Debate Panel answers

**Page 10:**

If you do nothing, the rise in obesity could cost the government a great deal of money to fund the medical expenditure a sick and ageing overweight population will require. Productivity of businesses will also be at risk due to the large amount of sick days caused by obesity-related health problems. This means the country's economy will suffer.

A national obesity and healthy eating awareness campaign can tackle the problem. However, your government will be in competition with the advertising campaigns that producers of unhealthy foods run to persuade consumers to buy their food. Is the govern-ment prepared to invest the millions of dollars required to spread the healthy eating and lifestyle message?

Putting a tax on unhealthy food to discourage people from buying it may work, but what about providing consumers with inexpensive, healthy alternatives? Will the government come up with agricultural policies which encourage the cheap production of fruit and vegetables so that even the poorest people can afford them?

**Page 16:**

In this situation you could:
- Reduce the fat in your products and promote this on the packaging;
- Offer collectible tokens on the crisp packets so that people can buy sports equipment for themselves or their schools;
- Fund research into obesity and obesity-related problems;
- Offer to fund healthy eating campaigns and work in conjunction with the government to encourage people to live healthily;
- Make sure that you promote your company's good works to consumers through advertising. This is to ensure that your profits from crisp sales do not drop because of the suggested link between your products and obesity.

**Page 23:**

You could ban sweets, crisps and similar foods from vending machines at your school and from the cafeteria. You could also ban such foods from the premises, so that students would not be allowed to have them in packed lunches.

However, these solutions may not be as simple as they sound. The consequences of a ban could be that the school would lose money – vending machine sales are often used to supplement school funds. More staff would be needed to check all of the children's lunch boxes and explain to parents why the food has been returned uneaten. This sort of action is likely to create some bad feeling.

An alternative policy could be to promote a healthy eating lifestyle to both children and parents through a series of workshops – for parents in the evening and for children within the school day. You could ensure that more healthy choices are offered in the canteen in conjunction with your healthy lifestyle education programme and only offer healthy foods in vending machines.

**Page 30:**

You could take your children to a doctor to set them some exercise, dietary and weight targets. You could ask for contact details of any support groups that help young people who suffer from being overweight. The whole family could learn about healthy eating, and then take part in shopping and cooking. A family keep-fit action plan could also help. This could include simple activities like walking to places whenever possible and some fun family activities at the local leisure centre too. Television time could be limited to a maximum of two hours per day, or used as a reward for exercising and eating healthily.

**Page 37:**

In developing countries, high levels of obesity are usually found in the cities. You could target city schools with a healthy eating message backed up by poster advertising campaigns on public transport and billboards.

Obesity in developing countries is a new problem; research and statistics are needed to get a true picture of how it is affecting people. You could ask the World Health Organization to help set up a programme of research in your country. You could also meet with sugar cane industry officials and union representatives and explain the purpose behind your campaign. You could point out that you will work with them to develop new markets and use for cane. You would also like them to research the growing of alternative and healthier crops for use within your country and for export, and your government will subsidize them to do so.

**Page 44:**

You could start by calling a meeting with local doctors and health professionals and inviting them to express their views, ideas and solutions to the problem. The issue should also be discussed with your local govern-ment councillors to make sure that they recognize the seriousness of the situation and are keen to help.

Such campaigns need additional funds and usually outside expertise. National governments and internation-al organizations such as WHO and the United Nations may be able to help as they will have significant experi-ence in this area.

The project will involve people at all levels in your city – health professionals; educators; those involved in sports and leisure; local shops; and of course the people themselves.

# Index

Page numbers in **bold** refer to illustrations.

advertising 40, 41, 47

blindness 4, 20, 32, 33, 36
body mass index (BMI) 4–5, 6, 8, 19, 25, 27, 46
bullying 31, **31**, 42

calories 6, 7, 8, 12, 14, 15, 16, 27, 30, 40, 46
cancer 4, 18, 20
central obesity measurement 6
children 8, 14, 15, 16, 18, 19, 24–31, 34, 35, 36, 40, 41
Common Agricultural Policy (CAP) 13, 39, 46
computer games 16, 30, 36
confectionery 4, 6, 7, 8, 14, 15, 23, 31, 43, 47
crisps 4, 14, 16, 23, 31, 43, 47
cycling 17, 27, 36, 38

dairy products 13, 44
developed world 9, 12, 32
developing world 10, 32–7, 47
diabetes 4, 18, 20, 31, 32, 33, 37
    Type 1 18–19
    Type 2 18, 19, 31, 33, 37
diet 4, 13, 18, 19, 20, **25**, **26**, 28, 36, 37, 42, 44, 45, 47

energy 6, 7, 8, 11, 25, 28
exercise 4, 7, **7**, 8, 16, 18, 24, 27–8, 30, 38–9, 40, **40**, 41, 42, 47

farmers and farming 13, 35, 39, 44
fast food restaurants 11, 12, 15, 38
fat 7, 8, 9, 12, 13, 15, 23, 26, 30, 31, 36, 37, 38, 40, 43, 44, 47
fat cells 8, **8**, 25, 26
food 6, 11, 12, 13, 15, 17, **26**, 29, 32, 39, 41
food labelling **42**, 43, 47
food producers 11–12, 14, 15, 38, 43
fruit 6, 13, 14, 15, 31, 39, 40, 41, 44, 45, 47

government action 11, 15, 38, 39, 40, 44, 47

health problems 4, 6, 18–23, 24, 27, 31, 38, 47
healthy eating campaigns 15, 41, 43, 44, 47
heart disease 4, 18, 19, 21–2, 38, 39, 43, 44, 45
high blood pressure 19, 21, 31

insulin 4, 18, 19, 20, 32, 46

junk food 14, 28, **29**, 30, 36, 38, 40

kidney dialysis 18, **19**, 20, 46
kidney failure 4, 18, 20

malnutrition 36, 37
men 5, 6, 7, 8, **34**, 35, 39, 44, 45
metabolism 17, 28, 46

North Karelia project 43–5

obesity and overweight
    causes of 11–17, 28–31, 35–7
        advertising 11, 14–15, **14**
        availability of food 11–12, 36
        birth weight 29
        bottle-feeding 29–30
        hereditary factors 17, 24–5, 28–9
        inactivity 16–17, 30, 35, 36
        modern lifestyles 12–13, 35, 36
        overeating 17, 29, 30, 38
        psychological factors 17
        snacking 14, **17**
        social and economic factors 31
    counselling 23, 28, 41, 44
    definitions of 4–5, 25
    drug treatments for 23, 28
    education 23, 40, 41
    financial cost of 22, 23, 24, 32, 33, 37, 47
    surgical treatments for 23, 28
    treatment of 22–3, 27–8

osteoarthritis 19, 22, 46

Pima Indians 37, **37**
psychological problems 17, 22, **22**, 27, 31
puberty 8, 25, 26

salt 13, 38
school meals 23, 40, 41, 44, 47
snack foods 14, 15
subsidies 39, 40
sugar 6, 12, 13, 31, 36, 37, 41, 43, 47
supermarkets and food retailers 11, 12, 38, 43, 44

taxes on food 10, 40, 47
television 4, 14, 16, 30, 36, 47
Trim and Fit Scheme 41

vegetables 6, 13, 15, 31, 39, 40, 44, 45, 47
vending machines 40, 41, 47

walking 16, 24, 27, 35, 36, 38, 47
weight-loss camps **10**
weight-loss programmes 23, 27, 28
women 5, 6, 7, 8, 22, 33, **33**, 35, 36
World Health Organization (WHO) 4, 6, 9, 26, 32, 44, 45, 47